By Richard Lewis

JOURNEYS
MUSE OF THE ROUND SKY
STILL WATERS OF THE AIR
OF THIS WORLD
THE PARK
THE WIND AND THE RAIN
OUT OF THE EARTH I SING
MOON FOR WHAT DO YOU WAIT?
MIRACLES
IN A SPRING GARDEN
THE MOMENT OF WONDER
IN PRAISE OF MUSIC

MIRACLES

Poems by children of the
English-speaking world

collected by

RICHARD LEWIS

Simon and Schuster, New York

"Fire" and "Fear When Coming Home on a Dark Country Lane,"
copyright © 1964 by Patricia Taylor.
Reprinted by permission of the author.

"A Cat," copyright © 1964 by John Gittings.
Reprinted by permission of the author.

"A Strange Place" by Peter Rake, copyright © 1963
by *The London Daily Mirror*.
Reprinted by permission of *The London Daily Mirror*.

"Wondering," "Hills," and "Spider" are from Elwyn Richardson's anthology *In the Early World*, copyright © 1965 by The New Zealand Council for Educational Research and are used with the kind permission of The Council and Mr. Richardson.

Published by Simon and Schuster
Rockefeller Center, 630 Fifth Avenue, New York, New York 10020
TENTH PRINTING
SBN 671-65049-1 Library
Library of Congress Catalog Card Number: 66-20248
Designed by Helen Barrow
Manufactured in the United States of America

*To the children who have
made this book a reality, and to
children everywhere who carry
within them a poem for all
men to live by.*

ACKNOWLEDGMENTS

I would like to thank the following persons and organizations for their generous assistance during the entire course of this book: Mr. L. A. Minnich and his staff of the U.S. National Commission for UNESCO; Mr. L. G. Machado, Mr. Roger Caillois and Mr. Milton Rosenthal of UNESCO in Paris; the staffs of the UNESCO National Commissions of Canada, New Zealand, Australia, the Philippines, Malaysia, India, Nigeria, Liberia, and the United Kingdom; the personnel of the United States Information Service; and many educational systems throughout the United States and abroad.

I would also like to thank the teachers, collectors and organizations who generously supplied the illustrations by children. A list of the artists and sources follows. Title page: a child from the elementary schools of Springfield, Illinois, Mrs. Lucille Bealmer, teacher. Page 11: Judy Hoffman, 9, U.S.A., supplied by Mr. Ashley Bryan, Art Center of Northern New Jersey. Page 13: Jennifer, 13, New Zealand, supplied by Mr. Elwyn Richardson and the New Zealand Council for Educational Research, from *In the Early World,* copyright © 1965 by the New Zealand Council for Educational Research. Page 17: 10-year-old child from New Zealand; page 27: 9-year-old child from Canada; both supplied by Mrs. Betty Nickerson from the Children of the World Art Collection. Page 41: Tim Ross, 8, U.S.A.; page 61 (right): Gordon Javna, 8, U.S.A.; page 61 (left): Thea Boughton, 9, U.S.A.; page 75: Arnold Zandonella, 9, U.S.A.; all supplied by Mr. Ashley Bryan, Art Center of Northern New Jersey. Page 85: Sue M., 9, U.S.A., from my personal collection. Page 103: Steven Brodkin, 10, U.S.A., supplied by Mr. Ashley Bryan, Art Center of Northern New Jersey. Page 119: 13-year-old child from Australia; page 133: 12-year-old child from Nigeria; both supplied by Mrs. Betty Nickerson from the Children of the World Art Collection. Page 151: Rita Ensey, 8, U.S.A., supplied by Obadiah Knight School, Dallas, Texas. Page 183: Bevin, age unknown, New Zealand, supplied by Mr. Elwyn Richardson and the New Zealand Council for Educational Research, from *In the Early World,* copyright © 1965 by the New Zealand Council for Educational Research. Page 195: Judy Hoffman, 9, U.S.A., supplied by Mr. Ashley Bryan, Art Center of Northern New Jersey.

Special thanks and gratitude to Mrs. B. Gelardin, Mrs. Pat Lehrman, Miss Ruth Lederman, Mrs. Dianna Galin, Miss Charlene Slivnick and Miss Margaret Covode—who all helped in the typing and the correspondence involved in this book; to the many persons who were so kind and helpful in the countries I visited—and to my friends in this country; to my family, for their understanding and love; to my wife, Nancy, who guided and aided me in so many ways.

And to my excellent editors, Richard Locke and Bob Gottlieb, my gratitude.

INTRODUCTORY NOTE

MIRACLES *is a book of poems by children. It is a book intended to be read as poetry, not as a sampling of precociousness. The writers come from an enormous variety of backgrounds, but they have this one thing in common: they are all children—no different from the ones we see every day jumping, singing, yelling, discovering—who, for the very brief moment of a poem, have spoken with the intense clarity, vision and artistry of the poet.*

My desire to collect the poems of children began in 1961, when I started teaching literature and creative writing in an elementary school in New York City. I organized these classes because I felt that children would respond to literature by expressing themselves in their own stories and poems. In time, my belief was supported by some remarkable work—writing whose depth of feeling and understanding revealed a poetic consciousness beyond my expectations. It seemed to me that the quality of the work had more to do with childhood than with the background or education of these particular children. Surely children in many parts of the world were writing poems of the same extraordinary quality. With this in mind, I decided to make an international collection.

The U.S. National Commission for UNESCO and UNESCO headquarters in Paris were kind enough to put me in touch with schools in eighteen countries where English was either the native tongue or an important second language, and in 1964 I embarked on a world tour that led me to many of the children whose poems appear in this anthology.

Some of these poems were written in school or in extracurricular meetings with interested teachers. Some were written out of school by children who had the encouragement of their parents; others by children who kept their secret notebooks hidden away. Some were dictated to parents or teachers by five- and six-year-olds who had not yet learned to write; in some, adult or literary influences begin to be felt.

Whatever the circumstances, wherever I went—to rural sections of Canada or New Zealand, to isolated villages in India or Kenya, or to bustling cities in Australia, England or the United States—I found that, given the right encouragement and understanding, children could and did write poems that invited serious attention as poetry. Indeed, the children's very limitations of vocabulary and grammar served much the same function as the deliberate restrictions of form that the adult poet uses to concentrate his vision.

All the poems are exactly as the children wrote them. I have made every effort to weed out writing that might have been "edited" by an adult or plagiarized, consciously or unconsciously, by a child. The only corrections made were in spelling. The punctuation and form of each poem is precisely as the child composed it. Most of the poems were written between 1961 and 1964. Neither the population nor the amount of poetry submitted by a given country were considered in making the selections. The poems were chosen for their quality alone.

I hope that this book will demonstrate the artistry of which children are capable when they are given the opportunity; that it will serve as a testament to the power and value of the poetic vision that is an integral part of childhood; and finally that, as all real poetry does, it will give delight.

R. L.

NEW YORK CITY
APRIL 1966

CONTENTS

MIRACLES

PRELUDE

Poetry

THIS IS A POEM

This is a poem about god looks after things:
He looks after lions, mooses and reindeer and tigers,
Anything that dies,
and mans and little girls when they get to be old,
and mothers he can look after,
and god can look after many old things.
That's why I do this.

Hilary-Anne Farley
AGE 5
CANADA

POEMS

In poems, our earth's wonders
Are windowed through
      Words

A good poem must haunt the heart
And be heeded by the head of the
      Hearer

With a wave of words, a poet can
Change his feelings into cool, magical, mysterious
      Mirages

Without poetry our world would be
Locked within itself—no longer enchanted by the poet's
      Spell.

Peter Kelso
AGE 11
AUSTRALIA

MY POEM

My poem is full of joy
And full of hope.
I love my poem.
I enjoy reading it
While I'm alone.
I forget my sorrows and
My happiness comes along.

Ethel Hewell
AGE 11
PHILIPPINES

ONE

Morning

A dawn wind blows
breath on my bed.
A red haze fills the empty sky.

Susan Morrison
AGE 11
AUSTRALIA

The morning mist
Creeps down from the sky
To engulf the blue hills
With its white softness

Geeta Mohanty
AGE 13
INDIA

THE DEW

Quietly, and softly it came,
And no one saw it.
When it came
It just passed through,
And then Quietly and Softly
It brought the Dew
No one felt it,
No one saw it,
So no one knew why it came.

Amy Epstein
AGE 10
UNITED STATES

AWAKEN

Dawn breaks,
The sun creeps upon the earth
Until it's towering high;
The earth awakes.

Cotton feet rustle,
Dishes rattle;
Still,
The silver grass slumbers.

Flowers let their fragrance out,
Trees sway to the chant of birds,
Squirrels ponder;
Still,
The silver grass slumbers.

Sally Bingham
AGE 12
UNITED STATES

The birds are singing music
because the sun is shining.
I look at the sun with my eyes
and pretty stripes come.

The dew-bubbles on the grass
        are tiny balloons,
                for spiders to play with.

The grass looks like lots of tiny trees,
                only littler.

Desmond Garton
AGE 8
NEW ZEALAND

THE SUNBEAMS

Sun, Sun do you know
You are beams in the flames,
With glowworms in the light
And bright yellow red
Sharp silver flames
Spinning up,
Like a big block of gold
The sun is a very magic fellow.

Linda Pidgeon
AGE 7
NEW ZEALAND

It's a sunny, sunny day today,
There's not a fluffy cloud in the sky.
The sky's all blue in a light blue haze,
The orange sun is shining as it stalks along the sea,
And leaves a shiny golden path, for me to walk along.

Sarah Gatti
AGE 10
NEW ZEALAND

The wind was bringing me to school.
And that is the fast way to get to school.
So why don't you let the wind bring you
To school just like me? And you will be
In school on time, just like I was.

James Snyder
AGE 6
UNITED STATES

It lies in the groove
as still as a statue.
It has a steeple point.
The initial of skyblue ink
is the only difference I can see
From my neighbor's pencil.

I walk to school
beside my friend.
Our gray-blue uniforms
as neat as the petals of a flower.
But all I see in difference is
that my girlfriend has another name.

Noelene Qualthrough
AGE 11
AUSTRALIA

TWO

Spring

When spring comes
I feel like a
Daisy just opening up into a new life.
I feel like running twenty miles
And taking off my heavy coat
And putting on a pair of sneakers.
I feel like I started a new life
And everything is better
Then it was before.
I get faster
In running and I can go swimming outdoors.
It feels like the smell of new flowers
And the animals
Coming up from their holes,
The birds coming back from their vacations.
I love spring.

Michael Patrick
AGE 10
UNITED STATES

A little egg
in a nest of hay.
cheep-cheep.
crack-crack.
a little chick
pecked his shell away
cheep-cheep.
crack-crack.

Tina Anthony
AGE 7
ENGLAND

I feel a bit happier
when I see a kingfisher
in the spring-green willows
and the oak-leaved ferns
by the lemon wood trees.

Clifton Roderick Foster
AGE 11
NEW ZEALAND

A tree is a base for poison ivy.

A tree is a wrinkled old man with wicked intent, scratching at
windows and scaring babies.

A tree is a lady in a new coat in spring, and nothing in winter
because she wanted too much.

Some trees are nonconformists but not very many.

A tree is a house where you don't have to pay rent.

A tree is a place to hide when you want to sulk, where they can't
find you.

A tree is like an old friend—it grows on you.

Vicky Williams
AGE 13
UNITED STATES

CORNWALL

I dreamt I heard the grass grow
And crickets sprung and whirred,
And children came with glass jars to catch them.
And they played in the tall sea grasses
Among the dry stone walls.
At the foot of the cliff the sea pounded and broke.

And tamarisk waved.
The fishermen mended their lobster pots
With tamarisk branches and fastened them
Down with hard, fishy, tarry cord, in carpet stitch.

Caroline Bond
AGE 13
ENGLAND

Flowers look like balls of wool
And small bunched up trees
They sometimes smell the wind
The earth and the worms
The dandelion is yellow
The daisy is white
The flowers have eight legs
They have big ears
    to listen to the wind
Flowers taste like ice
    jelly, and they are like
Steam rising in the air.

Peter White
AGE 9
NEW ZEALAND

MY FEELINGS

I am fainty,
I am fizzy,
I am floppy.

Paul Thompson
AGE 6
NEW ZEALAND

THE GRASS

The grass seems to dance,
It seems to walk,
It seems to talk,
It seems to like to
Have you walk on it,
And play with it too,
It seems to be stronger than you or I.

Warren Cardwell
AGE 8
UNITED STATES

CLOUDS

Clouds are like waves
Rolling into the sky blue cave.

Paul Kuramoto
AGE 10
UNITED STATES

THE MAGIC FLOWER

Once there was a magic flower.
He lived out in the cold;
He lived in the dark and cold.
So he spun and spun
Until he grew very hot.
The whole world grew hot.
Then,
Out came the magic flower!
It was spun out,
Just as I am telling you.

Danny Marcus
AGE 8
UNITED STATES

TREES

The trees share their shade with
       all who pass by,
But their leaves whisper secrets
       only to the wind.

Nelda Dishman
AGE 12
UNITED STATES

THE FIELD OF THE MICE
AND THE MARIGOLD

The wind of the marigold,
The flies of the American Bird,
The shamrocks of the stones,
The Lord of the Fieldmice,
The marigold's lavender,
The marigold of the shamrocks,
The mice of the round-a-gold.
The tractors of the storm
How the wind blows
The wolves howl,
While the moon moves
Along in the sky.
The wind blows people's hats off
And blows people's dresses up.
The Lord Mayor of the Dreams,
The mari-of-the-golds,
The Lord Mayor of the Golds.

Etain Mary Clarke
AGE 5
IRELAND

THREE

The Wind and the Rain

THE FLOWER

The wind is half the flower
Because it is in the flower.
The white flower is in the clouds.

Diane Cairns
AGE 10
NEW ZEALAND

WIND

The wind is like the yeast in bread.
It makes the clouds fluffy white not red.
It bakes them in the oven of the sky.
Then sets them loose. I wonder why?

Robert Tanaka
AGE 11
UNITED STATES

THE FOUR WINDS

Ride the four winds
Ride the four winds gallantly
Whistling there in hymns
Ride the four horses
Ride the four winds bravely
Swoop the blossoms from their reach;
Hanging on the old peach tree
Ride the four horses
Ride the four winds.

Shirley Gash
AGE 10
NEW ZEALAND

THE SCARED CLOUDS

The clouds are stuck and scared to move
For fear the trees might pinch them.

Hannah Hodgins
AGE 11
UNITED STATES

THUNDER

I hear
the drummers
strike
the sky.

Glenys Van Every
AGE 9
AUSTRALIA

A THUNDERY DAY

Soiled clouds hang;
A clap of thunder booms
Afar.
The air is hotly still;
Not a breath of wind and
We are restless.

A tree stands,
The monarch of the field,
Moving not a leaf.
Suddenly
The electricity of the sky
Flashes
And lets us glimpse
The counterpane of earth.
Clouds gather in a conference
And then the welcome rain
Comes pattering.

Susan Meader
AGE 10
ENGLAND

SPLISH SPLOSH

I feel
    drops of rain,
And it goes;
SPLISH! SPLOSH!
   on my head.
And sometimes it goes;
SPLASH! BANG! CRASH!
    on my coconut.

Stefan Martul
AGE 7
NEW ZEALAND

CLOUDS IN A WILD STORM

Flash goes the lightning,
    Rumble tumble, Rumble tumble, reply the black tossing clouds.
The clouds come down lower in a storm
    and rain falls like millions of middle sized waterfalls.
The clouds quieten down,
    and are not so angry; angry and black.
When I was small, my aunty said,
    "If you watch hard, you might see
Pixies with forks picking the clouds so the water can come out."

Darcy May
AGE 10
NEW ZEALAND

WIND IN THE TREES

The wind galing
Sounding like breakers rolling
And whales driving through waves
Their tails splashing the foam,
Fountains spouting from their blowholes
Above the glittering sea
That rushes, roaring onto the black rocks.

Robyn
AGE 7
NEW ZEALAND

A STORM AT SEA

A storm at sea is dangerous.
The wind blows as if it had
        no sympathy.
The sky suddenly darkens—
A slash of lightning crosses
        the sky.
Then a sound like a giant
Stamping his foot
        in anger.
A spray of tiny stars would
        come from the waves—
Huge blue-green hands
        with white fingers
Rise from the sea.

Delia Valentin
AGE 10
UNITED STATES

RAIN

It's watering time
In the gardens of Heaven
As raindrops tumble
On cities and towns.

Richard Drillich
AGE 9
UNITED STATES

RAIN DANCE

The pattering rain dances,
Like a lovely maiden,
Waltzing in the wind.
Blithe breezes stroke their harps,
As clouds leap in step with misty partners,
Trying to embrace the thirsty earth.

Barbara Krasnoff
AGE 9
UNITED STATES

See this beautiful rainy day
That waters the pretty flowers,
And washes away my hopscotch.

Alliene Grover
AGE 7
UNITED STATES

RAIN

The rain screws up its face
and falls to bits.
Then it makes itself again.
Only the rain can make itself again.

Adrian Keith Smith
AGE 4
NEW ZEALAND

Many shiver
in their bed.
A heavy rain
a wet rose.

Jocelyn Klein
AGE 11
UNITED STATES

RAINDROPS

Raindrops shimmer down dirty glass
And measle the window pane.
The raindrops glide—leaving a motionless road.
Raindrops fall breaking themselves to tiny china
and run away like blood.

Ken Dickinson
AGE 10
NEW ZEALAND

PEARLS ON THE GRASS

After the beautiful rain,
The rocks shine under the sun,
Like the droplets on the cobweb
Amongst the green, green grass.

Geeta Mohanty
AGE 13
INDIA

There is an umbrella
In the sky,
It must be raining
In Heaven
I have one prayer to say to God
Don't let it rain tomorrow.

V. Cokeham
AGE 10
ENGLAND

FOUR

Playing

THE CASTLE YONDER

Here!
Where do you go?

To the castle
With the fairies,
To the castle yonder
Built by my uncle the King.

Which?
Which castle?

That one,
Over there.
That one yonder
Built by my uncle the King.

Why?
Why do you go there?

Because it is bad.
I go with witches
To the castle yonder
Built by my uncle the King.

When?
When was it built?

Long, long ago
In the days of old
The castle yonder
Was built by my uncle the King.

How?
How was it built?

With a wave of the wand it was built.
But I must go now
To the castle yonder
Built by my uncle the King.

John Dudley
AGE 12
IRELAND

CREEP

Don't make any noise.
Creep! creep, creep, watchout.
Somebody's looking from a high above tree.
Crouch down in the long tangly grass.
Look all about you, there might be a
warrior following.
Creep, creep, creep.
There is the village far below.
Look down—now go and tell your village
what you saw.

Linda Kershaw
AGE 10
NEW ZEALAND

MIRROR! MIRROR!

As I look into the mirror I see my face.
Then I talk to myself.
Then I play like I am in jail.
I pretend that I am bad.
I pretend sometimes that I am on a stage.
I sing to myself. I introduce people.

Deborah Ensign
AGE 7
UNITED STATES

FALLING IN THE CREEK

[FROM A HIGH BANK INTO A SHALLOW CREEK]

I was very scared
I was very frightened
In the water was
    stony
The water looked like
    ice from the top
When the water shakes
I see little bugs which swim
    away from me.
And when the water splashes
It whistles like the wind
When the water calms
You hear a hushing sound
And that is me asking for air
    from the icy water

Iris Heke
AGE 10
NEW ZEALAND

TWO MILLION TWO HUNDRED THOUSAND FISHES

One cold, winter morning
I got out of bed
And went downstairs
And went outside
And went fishing.

I put in my line
And started to pull
And I pulled and pulled
And, after a while,
I pulled out:
Two million two hundred thousand fishes!

Then I remembered
To get them all home
I needed to have
Two million two hundred thousand wagons!

When I got home
I went to my mother
And my mother said,
"What shall we do with
Two million two hundred thousand fishes!"

My mother sat down
And she thought and she thought
And, after a while she got up.
She opened the window
And threw out:
Two million two hundred thousand fishes!

Danny Marcus
AGE 8
UNITED STATES

WHEN I LEARNED TO WHISTLE

I remember the day when I learned to whistle,
It was in Spring and new sounds were all around.
I was five or six and my front teeth were missing,
But I blew until my cheeks stuck out.

I remember walking up and down the block,
Trying to impress those that heard me
With the tunes and sounds that came from my mouth,
For I sounded much better than the birds in the trees.

I remember being hurt, for nobody seemed to care,
And then I met an old man who stopped and smiled.
He too blew until his cheeks stuck out.
He sounded just like me, for his front teeth were missing.

Gordon Lea
AGE 11
UNITED STATES

DANCING

Booming thundering sound.
The continuous booming of the drum.
Children start moving in stiff movements
A flicking in time movement, arms reaching, feet snapping
Bodies stiff.
The rhythm changes.
Sweeping, swooping, gliding
Relaxed.
Fingers trail through the air.
The drum ceases and movement stops. . . .

Alex M.
AGE 10
NEW ZEALAND

THE CONCRETE MIXER

Sand, shovel and shingle
Mortar,
Round mouth rattling,
Always being fed,
Always turning,
Spits out food,
Forever hungry.
Powerful,
Noisy,
A useful tool,
Three teeth.
Stark and ugly,
Silent
At day's end.

Timothy Langley
AGE II
NEW ZEALAND

THE MINE

Here are we; in the darkness,
Close to the very heart of Mother
    Earth,
Where her blood flows in seams of
    shining coal,
And our picks beat a rhythm to her
    heart,
Where her warm brown flesh encloses
    us
And her rocky bones trap us.

Bronwyn Mason
AGE 12
NEW ZEALAND

SCRAPYARD

Old, old cars, rusting away,
Some cars whole—in these we play.
Now I am swerving round a corner,
Streaking round a bend,
Zooming past the finishing line
To the checkered flag—
Finishing a perfect first,
Ready for the autograph hunters.

Michael Benson
AGE 11
ENGLAND

I WISH

I wish I was a train,
And I would roll along
      the streets.
Men would push me.

Roger Mortimer
AGE 7
NEW ZEALAND

BABY PLAYING

Someone's playing with a bottle,
And someone's playing Indians,
And the Baby's playing, too.

And someone's playing with a car,
And someone's drinking tea,
And someone's very naughty, too.

Roderick Crilly Clarke
AGE 5
IRELAND

PLAYING

When I was playing
I said to myself,
"I'm all alone
And no one comes."
So I go and see
What they are doing.

Pauline Costello
AGE 5
CANADA

FIVE

Summer

Summer is golden,
Summer is green,
The freshly cut grass.
Down, down, down, we go, from the peak of the hill,
ROLLING.

Gillian Sellers
AGE 9
ENGLAND

Lying in the sun
In midsummer
Looking at a blue sheet
Of happiness.
Only a breath of wind
To spoil it.

Ian Johnson
AGE 9
NEW ZEALAND

Inviting, rippling waters
Waiting for little toes
Hurry, go get changed!

Margaret Bendig
AGE 10
UNITED STATES

WHOOPS A DAISY

One nice summer day I heard a sound;
Boom, bang—a drum was playing.
I was standing on a branch
And it was hanging right over the pond
And I started to dance.
I sang a song at the same time.
The song went like this;
Tra la, boom, bang,
Tra li, tra la
And I jumped—whoops, splash
In the pond I went.
I kept singing the song
Tra la, crash, boom, bang, tra li
Over the trees I swing.
Tra li, tra la, boom, boom, bang, tra la, tra li.
I started to dance on my head,
And I made up another song that went like this;
Clang, splash,
    ging—gong,
        Whoops,
Clang, splash,
    ging—gong,
          2.X.P.
            Whoops a daisy.

Teddy Carr
AGE 8
NEW ZEALAND

RAIN

I love Rain
On a summer's day
When I have just been swimming
And the leaves rustle and the winds blow
And my mother calls
And says to get out of the water,
And we run home.
No animal seems to care
If it rains or snows
Or the winds blow
Oh I wonder why.

Leila Heron
AGE 8
UNITED STATES

TREES

The grass is a rug for the trees to
       dance upon;
The branches of the trees are arms
Gracefully pointing to the blue-pillowed sky,
Waiting for a partner.

Susan Forman
AGE 7
UNITED STATES

A KINGDOM OF CLOUDS

The heat of yesterday transformed the city into
A kingdom of clouds.
The skyscraper pierced the fog
looking like temples of an ancient land.

Maura Copeland
AGE 10
UNITED STATES

DUSK

The sunset bloomed
Like sunny balloons
On holiday streets.
The air was soft and silent.
Swept away
Were all ashes
Of a bright summer's day.
The moon
Took his place
At watching the silent, sleepy world
Slip by at his feet.

Eve Recht
AGE II
AUSTRALIA

SIX

Creatures

NIGHT AND NOISES

Loud nights and the creaking.
Barking voices of the dogs
       smelling around for
          fish bones.

Day comes.
The voice of a cow comes home
       for its calf.
Secretly walks through the mud
       trying to get back to its calf;
Leaning its head through
       The wĕta-eaten rails,
Trying to get back to its calf.

Rolling its brown glass eyes,
       Making a noise to make the
         calf answer back.

A man comes and lets the cow in
       looking in the hay pen.
The noise of the engine starts
and slowly driving the cow into the bales
To be milked and leg-roped with the rope.

Pulling the dull-colored calf along to have a suck.

Glennis Foster
AGE 10
NEW ZEALAND

SEAGULL

As I watch over
towards the jungle gym,
I see some thing.
It looks like a small hailstone,
girdled in its mangled perch
of jungle gym.
It's silent and so am I.
It suddenly slouches
and lets out
a loud half-squawking,
half-screaming yell,
then it wrestles a little
and heaves itself into the flared
sky
like a hawk
and I know it's a gull.

Shirley Gash
AGE 10
NEW ZEALAND

BLUE MOON BUTTERFLY

Mooned wings on the Blue Moon butterfly,
Dead!
In its crowded displaying grave
Lived a short life, now dead.
He struggled but it didn't do good!
Butterfly body
with two moons
of its own.
Blue, smudged on a black background.

Paul Williams
AGE 10
NEW ZEALAND

I LOVE ANIMALS AND DOGS

I love animals and dogs and everything.
But how can I do it when dogs are dead and
      a hundred?
But here's the reason: If you put a golden egg
      on them
They'll get better. But not if you put a star
      or moon.
But the star-moon goes up
And the star-moon I love.

Hilary-Anne Farley
AGE 5
CANADA

Silent logs floating
Statue still—
Sly vicious animal, a sinister monster.
Regiments of scaly armored troops
Drifting down the river.
Hot, damp, steamy jungles.
A brute of a creature
Flesh-eater, killer.
Icicle teeth, in a huge dark abyss.
A crocodile.

Michael Goodson
AGE 9
NEW ZEALAND

THE SPIDER

With black, wicked eyes, hairy thin legs and
                    creepy crawly movements
Black shoe polish coat shining dully.
Hairy black thin legs.
Beautiful, silky and soft web
Dew hangs like minature diamonds on lacy fingers.
A quick movement and this monster disappears.

J. Jenkins
AGE 10
NEW ZEALAND

THE JELLYFISH

Domelike top, speckled comets converging;
    Gold-green flesh, wave edges urging.
Jellylike globules, soft lattice arms,
    Spiked fury, leather-lash meting out harm.

Golden-smooth rods, waving whiplike with water,
    Beauty and danger, the jellyfish slaughter.

Glenn Davis
AGE 11
CANADA

A tadpole, a baby slyful tadpole
A tadpole, black and spotted tadpole
A tadpole of speed and slenderness
A tadpole with a glassy tail.

She flips her tail and flashes on,
She weaves her body about the weed,
And jerks between a sharp great stone.
She cuts the water of dirt and grit,
And dyes the water with jump and vigor.

She eats of weed, she eats of fly,
She eats with fish, she eats with friend.
At times of rest she sets her chest
Upon the bed of sand and stone.
Oh little tadpole, grow and grow again.

William Michael Taylor
AGE 12
ENGLAND

The clouds float by
with eaglets watching
by and by
Really watching.
They must think that they are kings
Those funny little bald things.

Jackson O'Donnell
AGE 8
UNITED STATES

A little white mouse
Playing upon a sunbeam
Then sliding back down.

Mona Thomas
AGE 11
UNITED STATES

THE RABBIT

I see a rabbit drinking at a stream,
I know it wants to run from me, tense
      as it may seem,
But some unknown force makes it stay
      right there and sit,
The same curiosity that makes me keep
      watching it.

Philip McIntyre, Jr.
AGE 12
UNITED STATES

DEW ON A SPIDER WEB

Two twigs acting as a loom
Hold a wonderful weaving.
Silver threads, simple but beautiful against the
       bright blue sky.
Who would ever think this was woven by an ugly
       old spider?
How I would like to have a wonderful weaving like
       that.
My one would never fade away.

Michael Stone
AGE 10
NEW ZEALAND

WILD SPURS

My rooster comes to me
On big eagle's feet
And goes away
On little horse's spurs
Guarding and watching
The strutting hens
That tear the ground
And get the worms.

Owen
AGE 12
NEW ZEALAND

WILD HORSE

With shiny skin
    And fiercest eye
Clattering hoof
    Will never die.

From memory of mine,
    The horse (if wild)
A creature fine
    Who's always bright

Yet man took horse
    To call his own
And broke him in
    With reins and such.

Man used a whip
    'Twas very coarse
And took the life
    From wild horse

That proud creature
    Jumping free!
Is now a sad and gloomy one
    Oh, think! of what the man has done

Wild, free
    Full of glee
That was
    The wild one!

Shame on man
    To do what's done
Took spirit, soul, all joy as well
    Oh—! wild horse!

Hillary Allen
AGE 9
CANADA

SPARROWS

Prr!
Mistress has put out the bread.
Now I can chase birds.
I'll creep towards them
And when I am near them
I'll watch them fly.

Prr!
Pussy the mighty am I.
Here I am,
King of animals.
I'll make the birds scatter—
"The great Lord Pussy is coming!"
They'll chirp.

Prr!
Here I go
Treading softly on my royal paws.
There flies the first bird,
A proud-looking blackbird.
He warns the other birds
And then up, up, he flies.

Prr!
None are left
But four common sparrows.
But what is this?
Are they blind and deaf?
Although I move closer
They do not take wing.

Grr!
Why do they not flee
From their almighty king?
They fluff out their feathers proudly,
And defiantly go on eating.
They seem to laugh at me.
Me! The king of animals!
Grr! Grr!

Anne Fyfe
AGE 11
NEW ZEALAND

A CAT

Silently licking his gold-white paw,
Oh gorgeous Celestino, for
God made lovely things, yet
Our lovely cat surpasses them all;
The gold, the iron, the waterfall,
The nut, the peach, apple, granite
Are lovely things to look at, yet,
Our lovely cat surpasses them all.

John Gittings
AGE 8
ENGLAND

SEVEN

The Sea

THE SEA

On the way I saw the sea,
The sea I saw on the way.
I saw a ship on the sea,
On the sea I saw a ship.
There were seagulls and birds
          on the sea
Seagulls and birds were
          on the sea.

I saw some pretty shells
a-lying on the bottom of
          the sea
I would have liked to pick
them up if I weren't in
          the train.

Suzanne G.
AGE 8
NEW ZEALAND

God makes ducks
      and rainbows,
And huts
      in the tree,
And traps
      for cats,
And skies that are blue,
And pretty ladies
      on the beach
Catching pretty butterflies.

Gary Wall
AGE 8
NEW ZEALAND

ON THE BEACH

The flour-capped waves
mash the sand.

Driftwood and people
tint the sand.

Cliffs darken the gray-green
with drab coats of shadow.

Cliffs salted with
bushes and caves.

Waves roll
slackly back.

Colin Parker
AGE 10
NEW ZEALAND

Out fishing on the ocean
The land a rocky ledge,
The surf whipping the boat
Like a prickle hedge of white roses.

Bretton Pollock
AGE 10
NEW ZEALAND

A gull's ghostly call.
Fish dive to deeper water
flashing down like leaves.

Stephen Hopkins
AGE 10
AUSTRALIA

The little fish cries;
His mother has been
Taken by
Nets.
He dives
To the bottom
Trying to forget.
His stillness makes
Him afraid.
He swims after his
Mother
Silently crying.

David Recht
AGE 10
AUSTRALIA

SKELETON

Skeleton of a fish,
        eaten up!
Bits of flesh all over the beach;
only bones to be left.
The tail,
        pulled off
        is lying on the golden sand
mirrored by shiny pane-glass water.

Shirley Barry
AGE 12
NEW ZEALAND

A LITTLE FISH

A little fish swims in the water
With the mummy fish. But camels don't
Go in water, and see the sun rising, a fish and the fish
Go right in their little house and snuggle up.
See the gold? I love the little fish!
I love them all.
But be careful when you swim in the water there might be fish,
Or even whales or alligators.

When the sun rises again and all is done
I love the little fish but what can I do?
The whales will eat them
And the sun goes up again.

Hilary-Anne Farley
AGE 5
CANADA

SLAVE OF THE MOON

The sea rushes up
To eat the muddy shore,
Slips back into the waves
To return once more.

Spluttering, foaming, frothing
Pulling at the land
Again it tries to eat
The dampened, salty sand.

But will it reach
Its destination soon?
Or must it always be
The slave of the moon?

Mary Yarmon
AGE 11
CANADA

HOW CAN THE SEA BE DARK AND GRAY?

How can the sea be dark and gray?
The sky is blue. The sands are white.
Winter has flown away.

How can the sea be dark and gray?
Is it thinking of something it saw long ago?
Of the changes it's seen from an early day?

Billows of foam pile up on the cliffs,
The rocky ledges are flooded, then dry.
The sun is shining bright above.
How can the sea be dark and gray?

Susan Harrison
AGE 11
CANADA

Waves slap on the shore.
And make noises like houses crumbling
many houses falling down.

Carol Moore
AGE 8
UNITED STATES

THE FLYING SEA

The sea rolls by.
It's like bombs exploding
And when the roll fades away,
The flying sea sings.

Roger Mortimer
AGE 7
NEW ZEALAND

THE SEA

The untamed sea is human
Its emotions erupt in waves.
The sea sends her message of anger
As the waves roll over my head.

Susan Shoenblum
AGE 11
UNITED STATES

THE PIER

One very nice day I went to the pier,
There were lots of noises that I could hear,
There I saw so many ships.
They were buzzing; buzzing, buzzing
I couldn't stand it, there was so much noise—
As if the place was full of naughty schoolboys.
However, I didn't want to leave. I had to be brave
Because I was enjoying myself, looking at the waves.
Soon I had to go; night had come, lights went on,
The day had brought me so much fun.
That night I could not sleep; I wanted to sing,
Of ships and waves and bells that ring.

Enrique Lozada
AGE 10
PHILIPPINES

SUNSET ON THE SEA

We sat there and watched as Pen, the sun god
In his fiery wrath drove his chariot behind a cloud
To give his horses water.
And waving purple and pink banners behind him
      were his servants in yellow cloaks
      and his wives in stunning scarlet.
He, in a cloak of glittering diamonds and gold,
      his pale blue horses, his wives, his servants,
Reflected their souls upon the sea.

Pen, the sun god, looked over his kingdom:
The coal-black sea; the fishes, purple, white and silver;
      the crabs; the eels, and me in my boat.
He smiled; a purple banner rippled and amidst waving banners
      pink dimples showed,
And he went from his chariot to his people beneath.

Lori Ubell
AGE 11
UNITED STATES

EIGHT

Autumn

Hours are leaves of life
and I am their gardener . . .
Each hour falls down slow.

Susan Morrison
AGE I I
AUSTRALIA

HILLS

Scrub hills,
> sheep-tongued, sheep-tramped hills
> > mountain hills,
> > > rabbiter hills:
The brown patches blind my eyes;
> scrub pointed out, like rows of trains
> > that drive along the rails.
Sheep happy,
> quietly eating.
> Starlings pick the ticks
> > off the patchy
> > > green hills.
> Twitchy heads move
> > up above the bluegum
> > > trees.
Sheep rub on the
> bark trunks;
> > dead gorse,
> > > live gorse,
> > > > growing on the hills.

Glennis Foster
AGE 10
NEW ZEALAND

TREE

Autumn has come and things begin
as the leaves fall off the tree.
Bare as can be and cold as can be
the trunk squiggles down.
Day by day, and night by night
the tree sways to and fro.
Morning begins, and things begin
as the tree trunk stays where it is.
It's nearly dead as it rots away
and nothing for it to care about.
It shrinks, twists, sways
as it's nearly ready to fall,
till at last its time has come
for it hits the mighty ground.
It's nearly daybreak
and the tree is still there
as it gradually crumbles away,
till at last it is gone
and nothing has begun
for that lonely tree.

John Hunter
AGE 12
NEW ZEALAND

A leaf looks prickly and sharp
And the leaf looks tickly
And the wind looks strong
And a leaf runs along the ground
and the wind

Peter Johnson
AGE 8
NEW ZEALAND

A leaf crashes gently to the ground
A cricket lands lightly on it
And tunes itself for a song.

Jennifer Hodgman
AGE 10
UNITED STATES

FIRE

Flickering flames of gold and red
Creeping forward like a cautious thief
Devouring greedily the old, dry twigs;
Wisps of light gray smoke
Floating higher and higher
In the damp air of the dawn.

Jill Craik
AGE I I
AUSTRALIA

FIRE

I am fire. You know me
For my warmth and light
For my crackling, leaping
Colored light
Which comforts all.
I am fire. You know me
For my endless moving,
Burning, destroying hunger
Which eats all.
I am fire. I have one foe
Who conquers my might,
Who quenches my thirst,
Who swallows my light.

Pat Taylor
AGE 13
ENGLAND

THE FICKLE WIND

The drowsy wind
Whispers a sleepy tune.
The whistling wind
Charms the enchanted leaves.
The savage wind
Roars a violent storm.
The weeping wind
Bleats—lonely and forlorn.

Cindy Schonhaut
AGE 8
UNITED STATES

I saw a green beetle climb crippled grass.
I saw the white speck of a dying butterfly.
I saw grass tops and seedy heads chatter and rustle.
I saw crippled grass bend oldly forward.
I saw yellow flowers in a buttercup wind.
I saw tinker-tailor grass bending in a greasy wind.

S. Kershaw
AGE 10
NEW ZEALAND

STILLNESS

The trees,
The long green weird grass,
The creek,
All still and quiet.

The wind rushes past
And disturbs the nature around.
The little yellow leaves speed up a little
As the wind pushes them down the creek.

As the breeze faints out,
The trees,
The long green weird grass,
The creek,
All turn still.

Maresala Leaso
AGE 12
NEW ZEALAND

FOG

Fog is a puff of smoke
Blinding and thick,
It's like a great god
Smoking a giant pipe,
The eyes of the people show little tears
From the thickening smoke.

Scott Ingbritson
AGE 9
CANADA

NOVEMBER

The birds have all flown
And I am alone
In the big sky's mouth.

Charles Gluck
AGE 10
UNITED STATES

NINE

People

GROWNUPS

Grownups are silly,
They never drink coffee
When it's served
To them.
They just talk
And never drink it
Until it's cold.
Isn't that silly?

I haven't grown
Since I was five
I haven't grown at all—
Grownups are just getting shorter.

Marc Duskin
AGE 10
UNITED STATES

THE TRAINS

As the train rattles along the bumpety rails,
The rails get angry in terrifying rage
As people enjoy the ride.
People look out of the windows and see the world.

Rosemary Spencer
AGE 8
NEW ZEALAND

A TEACHER

A teacher's got a temper
like a bull.
He growls and roars
like a tiger,
he stamps and gets mad
and sometimes he's glad
he did it.

Bruce McGregor
AGE 11
AUSTRALIA

SINGING

The children are singing,
their mouths open like sleepy fish.
Our teacher conducting the class
waves her arms
like a rhyme in water.
The girls sing high:
our ears ring for the sweetness.
Listeners stand in dazzling amazement.

Peter Shelton
AGE 10
AUSTRALIA

SOMEONE

And she looked at me,
Saying with her eyes,
A lie like she always
said a lie.
And I would listen

for truths when I
listened to her,
which was rare,
but when I did,
I would try to

hear truths but,
I would never
hear them,
I would hear
only lies...

Lee Jaffe
AGE 12
U.S.A.

HOUSEHOLD PROBLEMS

Tick-tock, tick-tock,
The sound of a clock.
You turn to the door
To answer a knock.
The children are fighting
Ooops there goes a sock.
Tick-tock, tick-tock,
The sound of a clock.
The chair needs mending.
The hinges need bending.
The boys are still fighting,
Now two things need mending.
Tick-tock, tick-tock,
Time goes with the clock.

Larry Haft
AGE 11
UNITED STATES

An empty bed
No arguments
No one to come home to

And all is dark
In day and night
I am all alone

Stephie Silon
AGE 10
UNITED STATES

WIFE AND HUSBAND

While the sun shines
Mother minds her work
And makes kind smiles
While he makes lines of signing papers.

Crystal Day
AGE 9
UNITED STATES

A BOY

A boy tried to get killed
He ran up and down the road
Until a taxi ran over him.
Why?
Because his mother fussed at him.

Benny Graves
AGE 6
UNITED STATES

SUN GOES UP

I love the juice, but the sun goes up; I see the stars
And the moonstar goes up,
And there always goes today. And the sun
Loves people. But one always dies.
Dogs will die very sooner
Than mummies and daddies and sisters and
brothers because
They'll not die till a hundred and
Because I love them dearly.

Hilary-Anne Farley
AGE 5
CANADA

WHISKERS

I like to feel my father's whiskers,
They feel so very funny when I try to kiss him,
But when he shaves it does not tickle,
But still I wonder what my mother does.

Jane Brown
AGE 8
UNITED STATES

MY UNCLE JACK

My Uncle Jack collects door knobs;
Door knobs here, door knobs there
Door knobs simply everywhere;
Six on the window, twelve on the door
There's hardly room for any more;
Door knobs on the light switch and on the wall,
My Uncle Jack has got them all;
Blue ones, green ones, yellow ones and red
And a row of gray ones on the bottom of his bed.

David Amey
AGE 10
ENGLAND

MADMAN

He was caged up—
Caged like a mad bull.
He had no friends
Except
The cold touch
Of steel
On the bars.

He was kept
Alive
By the warm touch
Of sunlight
Through the bars.

Bill O'Shea
AGE 10
AUSTRALIA

A MADMAN

A madman lives in a very special house,
A very special house.
He lives with others like himself
In a very special house.
As he walks along the street he calls out,
"Have you any food or drink for a madman?
I will not hurt you. I will not touch you."

Stephen Dawson
AGE 11
AUSTRALIA

WAR

Not bad, but miserable
Drenched in gray sadness
Lonely grief handed out to all.

Sarah Mason
AGE 10
UNITED STATES

RAIN

It's raining, raining all around
Especially in London town.
Splish! Splash! of children's feet,
Running down the London street.

Splash! on the window pane,
The old man gazes at the rain;
He sighs and turns away his head,
And wishes he was young instead.

Pat Williams
AGE 13
ENGLAND

OLD MAN

Old man, once sturdy as a mountain
Now fragile as a twig.
It is many years and many storms till a mountain is worn
But a twig can suddenly go snap.

Old man, whose white beard is tangled like a net
Meshed and tangled is he
Tangled like old yarn
But yarn can be snagged.

Old man, whose face is gnarled like an old tree
Gnarled and cracked his face is
Like a rotted tree stump
But a rotted tree stump can crumble to dust.

Old man, how many snaps can you withstand?
How much more snapping,
How long will this go on?
Before you too crumble into dust?

Jessica Siegal
AGE 13
UNITED STATES

TEN

Feelings

OH, JOYOUS HOUSE

When I walk home from school,
I see many houses
Many houses down many streets.
They are warm, comfortable houses
But other people's houses
I pass without much notice.

Then as I walk farther, farther
I see a house, the house.
It springs up with a jerk
That speeds my pace; I lurch forward.
Longing makes me happy, I bubble inside.
It's my house.

Richard Janzen
AGE 12
CANADA

I LOVE THE WORLD

I love you, Big World.
.I wish I could call you
And tell you a secret:
That I love you, World.

Paul Wollner
AGE 7
UNITED STATES

I am a nice nice boy
More than just nice,
Two million times more
The word is ADORABLE.

Martin O'Connor
AGE 10
NEW ZEALAND

KINDNESS

A loving arm
Shelters me
From any harm.

The shelteredness
Of kindness
Flows around me.

Mary Flett
AGE 9
NEW ZEALAND

WONDERING

As I lie here wondering
I feel an angry sweeping gust whirl around my legs.
The grass bustles about like a green jungle.
The leaves flap about,
As paper whirls around the playground.
The seagulls squabble over scraps
And look greedily for more.
Little insects crawl through the grass jungle
Like wild animals
In the small world I know little about.
I lie here wondering.

Kelvin Windsor
AGE 10
NEW ZEALAND

A STRANGE PLACE

A strange place
A place unknown
Only a stone's throw
From the Human race.

It is not deep
It is not wide
It is not tall.
Or small.

This place you shall never find
For it is mine and mine alone.
Strangest of all
No place is so unknown.

Peter Rake
AGE 12
ENGLAND

AN ENCHANTED GARDEN

Sometimes I think how lovely a garden would be
A garden in a cloud,
With raindrop flowers shining, snowflake
                  blossom drifting
And a tree with spreading frost leaves
A rainbow bridge across a stream,
And cotton-wool grass which is softer than any
                  earthly grass
It must be beautiful to dance there.

Carol Webb
AGE 9
ENGLAND

A WISH

I want to climb the santol tree
That grows beside my bedroom window
And get a santol fruit.
I want to climb the tree at night
And get the moon the branches hide.
Then I shall go to bed, my pockets full,
One with the fruit, the other with the moon.

Tomas Santos
AGE 7
PHILIPPINES

I feel relaxed and still
Heavy
As though I am floating—
Floating in mid-air.
When the sandman doesn't make up dreams for me
I see just pitch blackness.

Karen Anderson
AGE 7
NEW ZEALAND

I shook his hand
I touched him
How proud I felt.
He said "Hello" softly
I lost my voice,
But in my mind I said
     everything.

Ngaire Noffke
AGE 12
NEW ZEALAND

YOUTH

We stood together
Hand in hand.
He, so earnest, so concerned
In my tears.
Why do I cry?
What questions he asks!
Why do I cry?
How can I tell?

I could have laughed.
I could have stood
And screamed
At the dull drips of rain,
His fond stupidity.
His wiry hair,
His youth.
But no,
I stand and cry.

Anonymous
AGE 13
ENGLAND

BEING NOBODY

Have you ever felt like nobody?
Just a tiny speck of air.
When everyone's around you,
And you are just not there.

Karen Crawford
AGE 9
UNITED STATES

MY BRAIN

I have a little brain
Tucked safely in my head
And another little brain
Which is in the air instead
This follows me, and plays with me
And talks to me in bed
The other one confuses me,
The one that's in my head.

Annabel Laurance
AGE 10
UGANDA

SHADOW

My shadow is very bad and foolish
Wherever I go it follows,
I lash it, I whip it,
still it follows me.
One day I will kick it and it will never follow me.

Pramila Parmar
AGE 11
KENYA

THE DOORS

The doors in my house
Are used every day
For closing rooms
And locking children away.

Brian Andrews
AGE 10
AUSTRALIA

HURTING

It doesn't hurt no place when I'm sad
I just know I'm sad.

Benny Graves
AGE 6
UNITED STATES

I DON'T MIND

I Carolyn Jackson am a pure-blooded Negro in soul and mind.
My mother's from North Carolina and my father's from Florida.
I know when I go to that old wooden bed,
Somewhere on the other side of town, there is a child being
          put to bed in a soft cuddly nest.
But being a Negro isn't so bad (if you know what's going on)
Down South my cousin is being beat up—
And Look There . . . My aunt got put in jail for drinking from
          a white fountain.
But here I feel better because I have more freedom.
When I ride the train and sit next to a person of the
          opposite race
I feel like a crow in a robin's nest
And I feel dirty.
I'm not prejudiced or anything . . .
If we go on a trip and they call me names,
I Don't Mind.

Carolyn Jackson
AGE 11
UNITED STATES

THE MOUTH AND THE BODY

I passed along a quiet street
The mouth said a word
A man came and beat me
The mouth abused a lady
I was imprisoned.

Mouth, mouth, mouth
Always you act and I'm repaid
Once we shall meet
In a boxing ring
Then you start speaking and let me react
And you'll feel what I feel.

Philip Mwanikih
AGE 14
KENYA

I wonder
how God lives
in heaven,
when the clouds
seem to be collapsing
like broken birds.

Jewell Lawton
AGE 8
AUSTRALIA

TIME

The car stands still
As if it had never been driven.
People walk with their prams,
A dog runs down with a grin on his face.
The cross on the church reminds you of
happy days
While seagulls stick their tummies
out like heroes.

Reg Cowie
AGE 8
NEW ZEALAND

The eye penetrates into the thoughts of others,
Revealing like a human X ray;
But the eye senses feeling,
Releasing hurt and fear from beneath the outer shell.
The eye lets loose guilt
Quickly revealing shame.
The eye cries,
Showing deep pain.

Steven Terry
AGE 10
UNITED STATES

THE STATION

I am . . .
Down by the station, the old railroad station,
Where the floors are colored with ground-in dust;
The benches moan with tired, brief creaks,
Their metal legs eaten by rust.

Outside . . .
The dirt-brown stairs bake in the sun;
The paint on the walls is peeling.
Four rows of track gleam . . . and smell
Metallic and fresh—yet worn.

And . . .
You can see the heat as it patterns the air,
The blue of the sky softly rests on the roof.
All this to see, and no one to see it;
There's no one—no one but me.

Wondering . . .
The cars without the drivers,
The benches without their occupants,
Wondering at the empty loneliness of the place,
Which somehow might be filled.

John Rathe
AGE 12
UNITED STATES

THE DESERTED HOUSE

I am afraid—
For I am alone
In the deserted house
That stands tumbledown
In the wood
Everywhere is silent
So silent
You can hear
the silence hanging in the dark air
What was that
That noise! an owl?
I steal outside
To see if anyone is there
No! the wood is still
But the trees seem
To crowd closer
I tremble
I run back inside
Like a streak of lightning,
but inside is even more frightening
Than the wood outside
it's not exciting any more
I'm scared
My heart pulses and
Beats fast
I'd better get home
Now!
Before the empty
Or is it empty?—house
Gets me. . . .

Julie Fairbun
AGE 9
ENGLAND

FLEEING TO SAFETY

Under the force
Of a Sunday breeze
A Sunday breeze
And the humming waves,
We on a raft of wood
Dancing along
The ocean flood,
To reach,
Far away, our goal,
Away from
The hated souls,
Among God's harmless creatures.
We, on a wooden raft,
A wooden raft
A wooden raft.

Rajiv Chettur
AGE 10
INDIA

ARE WE THEIR EQUALS?

Time.
Is it everlasting?
Or can it be destroyed.
Perhaps.
Wind.
Are we its equal?
Have we yet conquered?
Can we conquer?
I think not.
Ocean
Is it not stronger?
Has it not smashed us?
?—I don't know.
Time,
Wind,
Ocean,
Are we their equals?

Helen Geltman
AGE 12
UNITED STATES

THE MEMORY-FILLED HOUSE

Along the long, dark hallway,
Up the memory-filled stairs,
Walking down the back way,
In the bare kitchen, with a harshness in the air,
In the dining room, no table or chair,
On the sideboard, no apple, orange, or pear,
In Grandma's room, no pictures on the wall,
Again, down the long, dark hall.

Margaret White
AGE 10
CANADA

MURDER

The house was haunted like spear
My heart was underground
My arms straightened in the fear of death
Everything tumbled in my eyes
Till I felt lead stick in my chest
Till I felt danger
Crushing into my heart
It was the black panther
With dripping spits of fever
Out of his germy mouth
Now no longer I could see the earth
My eyes closed gently
    and slept.

Peter Milosevic
AGE 10
AUSTRALIA

MY OLD GRANDFATHER

My old grandfather is dead and buried.
An orange tree was planted over his grave.
The tree fed on him and grew taller.
The oranges grew ripe and ready to drop.
The wind came and blew them off.
I came, picked them up and ate.
O what a dreadful thing!
I ate my poor grandfather's body.

Joseph Alumasa
AGE 14
KENYA

DEATH

Who set that endless silence
Of her breath?
Death is but death.
Death is like the growing of people
It cannot be stopped.

John Erwin
AGE II
AUSTRALIA

LONG SLEEP

When I die I think,
I'll think at first of brightness.
Red lines, blue lines, yellow lines,
Bright circles
Spots all dashing, speeding
Splitting across my mind.
Pushing, pushing me back over a ledge of doom.
Down, falling, falling
Into a pit of cold black endless darkness.
Everything goes in circles,
It's hot but it's cold
And then I stop,
I stop on a rock,
A rock as cold as ice.
But I feel that everything keeps going,
Going forever,
I feel at home.
I sleep forever
But everything just keeps going and going and going.

David Short
AGE 1 1
UNITED STATES

Dark, dark night.
The trees. The river.
One more day;
For so slow goes the day.
Before the end
    the world goes round
        once more.
The world begins the day.
The night has gone.
The day for the end of the world
    once more begins.
Once more begins the sun
Slow, so slow.
Go on, world, live.
Begin, sweet sun.
Begin, sweet world.
The people live and die.
    people die alive
       alive
           alive.

Lynette Joass
AGE 12
NEW ZEALAND

ELEVEN

Winter

WINTER

Winter stalks
At a steady pace.
Being sullen in choosing
The weather of tomorrow
The sour, chilly breeze
Sweeps the showery sky

The pods of rain
And minced mud
Bring forth a wintry day.

Gillian Humphrey
AGE 10
NEW ZEALAND

THE SLEEPY DAY

It was a silent day, the trees didn't move
Nobody bowed to the wind, the sun didn't rise
The cold breeze blowed.
It was a naughty day that didn't wake!

Harji Patel
AGE 11
KENYA

Fluttering helplessly
Buffeted, the bewildered starling
Pecks and shivers.

Thea Boughton
AGE 11
UNITED STATES

I stand under the naked tree,
Shuffling my feet among skeleton leaves.
The bark,
Aged and blurred
Color freckled and patchwork patterned.
Tangled branches reach skywards.
Twigs spindly and brittle
Fragile lace against the winter sky.

Linden McCall
AGE 10
NEW ZEALAND

Walking into the woods I see
maple sap dripping on the ground
I hear the cold crisp wind.
The night is black and cold
And I see a fawn listening to all of it
in his dream. . . .

Jill Bender
AGE 10
UNITED STATES

WINTER

Animals are restless
Birds are in flight,
Butterflies are not out.
Leaves; a gray blanket,
Winter lurks near.

Icy fingers grasp the world.
Snow falls; graceful, beautiful,
                    undisturbed.
Silence creeps about.

John Constant
AGE 10
CANADA

SNOW

There's a chime in the glitter of the snow,
There's a song of the frost, there's a whistle of the ice.
In the breeze there's a gentle blow.
The sun—it's lost. Winter is nice.

The birds have a wanting to fly,
I can hear their cry.
The wings have a sound.

The winter has snow piled on high,
All is white on the ground,
All is white in the sky.

Karen Orendurff
AGE 10
UNITED STATES

HAIKU

First snowstorm romp . . .
Her puppy's wet kiss
Froze on my sister's glowing cheek.

David Lippa
AGE 13
UNITED STATES

Slowly melting, slowly dying
My heart drops with the drips
The long finger of ice stretches out
And its tears roll off its tip.

Dianne Hill
AGE II
ENGLAND

LOST

He lost it over the dark gray hills
Of wonder—
Where the fingerless oaks grow;
Where the fruitless orange groves blow
In the merciless
Hungry
    Wind.

It must, by now,
Be torn
Between
The lush brown Earth
And the raging winter sky.

The wind must have
Dragged it
Over Moors,
Fields and Mountains
While he was at home
Enjoying his pipe.

Eve Recht
AGE 11
AUSTRALIA

TWELVE

Night

THE SETTING OF THE SUN

A streak across the sky
    Tells me that the sun
        Has finished its day.

The air gets colder
    As I watch the night
        Fold in.

It's like watching a deer come to drink
    As swift as can be.
        And . . . as beautiful as anything
          in the world.

A special sunset
    Just for me.
        The warmth inside me went
          out to greet it.

Maura Copeland
AGE 10
UNITED STATES

BREEZE

Gentle as a feather
Cat quiet
Snow soft
Gentle, gentle as a feather
Softer than snow
Quiet as a cat
Comes
The evening breeze.

Marie Hourigan
AGE 11
AUSTRALIA

NIGHT TIME

The color is dark blue,
In the sky the moon is up.
And the stars
I hear
Wind in the chimney pots,
And pit-a-pat on the stairs,
And babies crying.
It is quiet—
I feel lonely and sad.

Paul Wisdom
AGE 7
ENGLAND

SPIDER

Cold snuggle.
Not a sound.
Cold struck its woven-webbed bed
Which curled round and round.

Cold struck its cornered bed
Night covered in darkness
              Black.
Buzzing insects
Struck its wedded bed,

But too cold for the helpless spider.
He sat there.
Not a move;
Thin-sticked legs were shut away.

Raindrops fell;
The night grew colder . . .

Mavis Ruth Foster
AGE 12
NEW ZEALAND

A moth flies round the window
It sounds like silver paper.
A sixpence shines on the dressing table.
The dim light of the candle goes out
It is all dark.
All but the crack under the door
That shows little light
Soon it goes out.
The sixpence still shines
The moth still beats.

John Bairstow
AGE 8
NEW ZEALAND

VISIT

I saw it come across our lawn.
It had silently
stealthily
climbed our wall
and now stood
like a statue of stone
dressed in dark and mystery.
The air was old.

Eve Recht
AGE 11
AUSTRALIA

Dark fills the sky with his big black cloak,
You never hear him come
One by one the stars peep through,
Out comes the moon like a big yellow egg.

Beverley Dinsdale
AGE 9
NEW ZEALAND

The full moon whispered to the world
A word of wonder.
Then unfurled the light which lit the land
And lured the owls up to its hand.

John Rathe
AGE 12
UNITED STATES

Hungry tree!
Your knife branches
Cut the pie-moon into tempting pieces.

Nathan Altshuler
AGE 13
UNITED STATES

WITCHES

A star-white sky
Trees rustling as the wind lulls them to sleep
Shadowy creatures slinking through the grass
Clouds sailing,
Tattered and torn
Ragged and ripped.
Suddenly
In the sky
Soaring
    Zooming
        Diving about
            Flittering
Swooping into the air
Come witches
Cloaks ragged and torn
Streaming behind.
Cackling, laughing
Fading into the darkness.

Linden
AGE 10
NEW ZEALAND

FEAR WHEN COMING HOME
THROUGH A DARK COUNTRY LANE

On dark nights on lone country lanes
Why do you pester me so?
Why do you make me go
Creeping and crawling along
When the wind rustles in the trees,
Or when the owl hoots his nightly song?
Why, when mice scuttle as they please
Across the beaten track,
Do you make me stop or look back?
Oh! heartless thing, have you no feeling for me?
I wonder, I wonder,
Is it your nature so to be?
Is it your nature?

Patricia Taylor
AGE 13
ENGLAND

THE WITCH

A witch went into the forest
    Down
        Down
           Down
Into the deep deep forest.
Picking lots of mushrooms in the
    Deep
        Deep
           Forest.
And the wood is very still
And the witch flew into the forest
To make many spells.
Now she's making them
Nasty wicked spells
Making all the people
    Turn
To lots of pigs.
In the
    Deep
        Deep
           Forest.
Now she goes home
To make quite sure
They have
           Worked.

Patricia Thornton
AGE 7
ENGLAND

CANDLES

The candle screamed with fury,
Hot tears trickled down her face.
With figure slumped,
She slowly dwindled into shadows
Darkness!

Susan Heitler
AGE 11
UNITED STATES

WHAT'S NIGHT TO ME

Night is a beautiful thing,
One big black ball
As the clouds push it around.
Sometimes I think I am being rolled over by it.
Sometimes I think it's smiling at me.
The moon is the nose
The stars are the mouth.
And it is drinking the Milky Way.
Sometimes I dream that it will swallow me.
Night is the time for dreams.
Not day dreams but night dreams.

Sam Gilford
AGE 8
UNITED STATES

It was midnight
The sky was dark black
The stars were threepenny bits
The sea was making a sound
Like a silk dress.

Linda
AGE 8
AUSTRALIA

SLEEP AND DREAMS

Go perfect into peace,
    Peace mighty-majestic and molded, mounted
    Upon the satin whipped waves of the heavens.
    Roam in orchards of twilit apples, and
    Drawn by a million vermilion stallions,
    Shadow dappled across the fields of legend—
Go perfect into peace.

Go perfect into peace,
    Grave and golden,
    Free of fiery fury.
    Bathed in the glowing tears of dawn,
    Night-washed, night-webbed—
Go perfect into peace.

Peter Kelso
AGE 11
AUSTRALIA

THE NIGHT

As I curl up to go to sleep
I have such lovely thoughts
The darkness of my room,
The warmness of my bed
And what the day has brought.

Amy Goodman
AGE 11
UNITED STATES

The darkness darts. The moon curls up
Everybody goes to sleep, the stars come here
The stars dance all over the place.
Every daylight candlelight and candles go out.
They have tea before they go to bed.
The darkness stays until the morning
Then the darkness goes and the sunshine comes.

Janine
AGE 4
ENGLAND

Date Due